German *My Way*

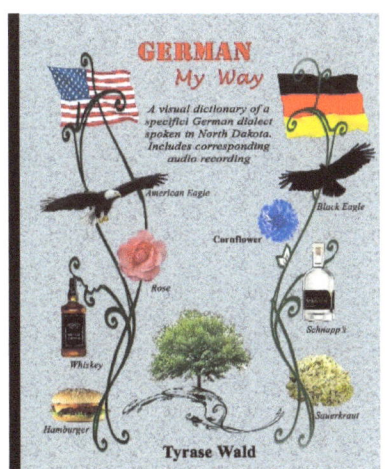

Copyright © 2019
(author *Tyrase Wa*ld and publisher *Husky Publishing*)
Cover Design © 2018 Jayne Flaagan
ISBN-13: 978-1-944410-23-0
original publication:2011

All rights reserved. No part of this publication may be reproduced or transmitted in any form or by any means, including informational storage and retrieval systems, without permission in writing from the copyright holder, except for brief quotations in a review.

NOTE: A CD recording of this book is available for purchase.
The CD is an audio recording of the author reading the entire book.
If interested, please email Husky Publishing at: djflaagan@gra.midco.net to request a copy of the CD. The purchase price for the CD is $14.95, which includes shipping and handling.

Contained in this book are many of the words (as well as their definitions) of a specific German dialect that I grew up speaking. In my own voice, I have also recorded these words so that one can hear their correct pronunciation.

The following is a small piece of the story behind the origin of this dialect:

Catherine the Great had established German colonies on the Volga and about 40 years later, in 1804, Czar Alexander I invited foreigners, especially the Germans, to settle on the steppes of New Russia. The first settlers came from Alsace and the Rhineland, with others following from Switzerland.

Hundreds of families had emigrated from South Germany in 1803 and 1804 and a second large wave arrived in 1808 from Lower Alsace, the Rheinpfalz and Baden, on the steppe above the Black Sea. The Liebental, Kutschurgan and Beresan settlements were among the settlements established.

Due to *"La Grande Fuite"* (the Great Flight) of 1793, a mass flight of tens of thousands of Alsatians left their homes to seek refuge in Germany. This was due to the turmoil and danger their lives were put in because of the French Revolution, when Alsace was a "foreign province" of France.

During campaigns against the Turks, Catherine II obtained for Russia a large territory which became known as "New Russia," then later as the Ukraine. In 1770 most of the Turkish fortresses were overtaken and several years later, Russia gained control of the Black Sea. Many German colonies were later established on the Jedisan steppe, which was between the Kutschurgan and the Beresan.lower falls of the Dnieper at the beginning of the nineteenth century.

A distinct dialect of the German colonists in South Russia consisted of three major enclaves in the Odessa area, namely the Catholic mother-colonies of the three Catholic districts of Liebental (Mariental, Josefstal and Kleinliebental), Kutschurgan (Selz, Kandel, Baden, Strassburg) and Beresan (Landau, Palatinate) and the Alsatian villages of Mannheim, Elsass, and Franzfeld. This is the dialect that I consider *"my German."*

Tyrase Mack Wald, author

Dedication

This compilation is dedicated to all who cherish this dialect and enjoyed the review of it.

ACKNOWLEDGMENMTS

My german language is the fabric and thread of my life. It is easier for me to communicate in german.

For instance in my dialect it is much faster and shorter, for instance to say "Do you agree with me?" We just say "gell?"

The following people are appreciated for giving me input, or just letting me check a few words with them.

- Mary Lyn Axtman
- Lizzie Bohn Wald
- Fr. Joseph Senger
- Bro. Placid Gross
- Fr. Ray Courtright
- Msgr. W. Vetter
- Mary and Clara Ebach
- Theresia Wolf
- Bill Wald
- Caroline Wald Moser
- Fran Ziegler Carroll
- Sr. Lorraine Kraft
- Mary Merck LaDuke
- Clara Mack
- Irene Gange Sunstrom\

Profound gratitude to Sandra Roth.

This work has been in progress for many years. New words from the past have been creeping in so it was difficult to bring the list to a close. It kept emerging.

Since the final copy I have another 25 words that I should have included. Maybe in the future there will be another attempt to recover these words of my past in another compilation of my dialect german.

Tyrase Mack Wald

Dialect German to English and Book German

By Tyrase Wald

English	Dialect	Book German
A little	bissel	in bisschen
About	ung geh fahr	ung geh fahr
Above	ovah	über
Absent minded	lichte sinish	lichte sinig
Accomplished	aus gemacht	aus gemacht
Accordion	hondargel	Zichharmonica
Ace	aus	das As
Accustomed	gehvand	
Admit	einlassa	einlassen
Adopt	on nema	adoptieren
Adorn	shan mache	verschonern
Affair	leeb shoft	lieb schaft
After	nogh herr	danach
Again	veeta	wieder
Against	dah geh	da gehen
Against	vay dar	da gehen
Agnes	Ung gah naise	Agnes
Agree	gel	zustimmen
Ahead	farshicht	nah voren
Ahead	fore	voran
Air	luft	Luft
Alike	gleich	gleich
Alive	la vend ich	lebendig
All Around	gringel room	rund herum
allow	dahr iff	erlauben

Almost	by noah	beinahe
Alone	ah lon ich	allein
Alphabet	boo shtaba	Buchstabe
Already	shoon	schon
Also	ah	auch
Altar	altaar	Altar
Alter boy	mes deener	Minestrant
Although	doch	obgleich
Always	immer	immer
lamb	shay fel	Lamm
Ambulance	dotewagen	Krankenwagen
Angel	angel	Engel
Anger	tsarn	Verärgert
Angered	ar rig art	verärgert
Angered	fartsanned	veräargert
Angry	base	boese
Animals	fee ich	Tier
Announce	far kind	verkiunden
Another time	annermol	ein anderes mal
Ant	oomas	Ameise
Anthill	oommah shah haufa	
Ants	oom ma tsah	Ameisen
Anvil	ambose	Amboss
Any	on ray	irgendein
Anywhere	irgent voo	irgendwo
Apple	aw ph ful	Apfael
Appetize	appatit liche	das verlangen
April	up ril	April

Approximately	un ga far	ungefahr
Apricot	ab brig gosa	Aprikos
apron	schurtz	Shürtz
Are	bish	bist
Are	sind	sind
Arm	aw rum	Arm
Armoire	shonk	
Around	droom	um
Around	gring gel rum	rund herum
Ashamed	sham ah	beshämt
Ashamed	ge shemt	beshämt
Ask	fro ah	fragen
Asleep	shlofen	schlafend
Attached	on gah vak sah	unbeveglich
At that time	sell ah mol	damals
Attitude	gniff	Einstellung
Auction	versteiger	Versteigerung
Auger	verbohrer	Bohren
August	aug goost	August
Aunt	bassel	Tante
Aunt	geddle	Tante
Autumn	sh pote yohr	Herbst
Award	fer goot ung	verutung
Awkward	ongshickt	ungeschickt
Away	avec	weg
Awful	au r rich	furchtbar
Awful	shreck lich	shrecklich
Awning	schirmdach	Wagendecke

Baby	kind	Kind
Back then	sel a mol	damals
Back	hinner room	zurück
Back	zurck	hinter
Backache	greizveigh	rückenschmerzen
Backward	hinn ar shicht	rückwärts
Bacon	shpeck	Speck
Bad	schlectes	schlect
Bad	bose-schlect	schlect
Bad	schlim	schlect
Bad	shlect	schlect
Badger	dachs	Dachs
Bag	doot	Tasche
Baker	bocher	Bächer
Bald head	blutt kopf	glatzkopf
Bald	blute	Glatze
Bale	bundle	Bündel
Ball	balla	Ball
Baptise	dah fah	Taufe haut
Bare naked	foo sell naugich	nack bis auf die
Barefoot	bar fees ich	barfuss
Bareheaded	horkepfich	barhäuptig
Barley	garscht	Gerste
Barn	russel beim	Stall
Barn	shtahl	Stall
Barrel	fessel	Fass
Barrel	shtond	Fass
Barter	veksel	tauschhandel

Barter	veksel	im naturaleien bezahlen
Bashful	blade	schüchtern
Basket	corrup	Korb
Bat	shpeck mouse	Fleddermaus
Bath	bawda	ein Bad
Bathing tub	bat kivel	Badewanne
Bead	grell	Glasperle
Beak	schnabel	Schnabel
Bear	bar	Bärr
Beat	schlagen	schlagen
Because of	iver dem	wegeb den
Because	daroom	weill
Bed wetter	bate sy ich her	betnässer
Bed	bate	Bett
Beer	bier	Bier
Bees	eema	Biena
Beet	rhode ribba	Rote rüben
Beg	on halt ah	betteln
Begrudge	fergonnen	vergönnen
Behind	hinner	hinter
Behind	hinner room	dahinter
Bell	gloke	Glocke
Belly	bauch	Bauch
Bench	bank	Bank
Bend	biegen	beugen
Beside	nah vah	neben
Beside	nevetz	neben
Bet	vayta	wette

Better	besser	besser
Between	tsvicha	zwischen
Bib	drulappel	Lätzchen
Bib	drule shartzle	Lätzchen
Bible	beebleskuischt	Bibel
Bigger	graiser	grözer
Bill	schnabel	Schnabel
Bind	binna	binder
Bird	fogel	Vogel
Black	shwartz	Schwarz
Black bird	schwartza fogel	Amsel
Black horses	raw bah	Rappe
Blemish	pfoot sah	Fleck
Blind one eye	shehl	Blindganger
Blindfold	augen verbinda	Augen verbinden
Blister	blow dar	Blose
Blood	blude	Blut
Bloodhound	blute hund	Bluthund
Blow	blohs	Schlag
Blow	blosen	Blosen
Blue	bloha	Blau
Bluing	blay	Bleiche
Boar	hatch	
Board	brett	Brett
Boat	shiffel	Boot
Bobbin	shpule	Spule
Body	caar rop ar	Korper

Boil (skin)	ah sah	Mulde
Bolts	shrawba	Schraube
Bone (small)	knech el	Knöchel
Bone	gnoch ah	Knochen
Bonnet	buhn net al	Kind kappe
Book	booch	Buch
Bookcase	buchershank	Büchershrank
boot	sh tiff el	Stiefel
boring	long vile ich	lang weiglig
Botched	forpfooshed	verhunzen
Both	all zwei	beide
Bottle	flaush	Flasche
Bough	nasht	Zweig
Bouquet	blooma	Bouquet
Bow	sloopf	Spange
Bowl	shee sell	Schüssel
Boy	boo	Junge
Bra	lie vel	Bustenhalter
brace self	sh tibe ar ah	versteufybg
Bracelet	armband	Armband
Bragger	gross gosch	angeben
Braid	pf lech ta	Pflechen
Brain	harn	gehrin
Bran	glye ah	Kleie
Branch	Zweig	Ast
Brassier	ly vel	Büsten halter
Bread	brodt	Brot
Break	brecha	brecjem

Breath	sh now fah	Atemzug
Breathe	schnauf	Atem
Breathe	shnow fah	Atem holen
Brick	backastein	Backsten
Bride	hoch ziterah	braut
bridesmaid	lod mod el	Brautjunger
Bridge	brig	Brüche
Bridegroom	hoch zitar	hochzeitar
Bridle	zaum	Zaumzeug
Broken	ferbrocha	Zerbrothen
Brood	breed lah	Bruthenne
Broom	Bessa	Besen
Broth	bree ah	Brühe
Brother in law	shvoger	Shwager
Brotherly	bruderlich	Brüderlich
Brush	barsht	Bürste
Bubble	blaze sell	Blase
Buck brush	hay kah	Unkraut
Bucket	armmar	Eimer
Bucket	keevil	Eimer
Buckle	schnall	Schnalle
Buffalo	boofelox	Büffel
Bug	kef far	Käfer
Buggy	boaggy	Kinder wagen
Build	Bauah	gebäut
Building	gah bye	Gebäude
Built	gebaut	gebäut

Bumbler	yokkel	
Bump	gnew bah	stoss
Bundle	bundel	Bündel
Bungle	hoodel	verhunzen
burn	brenna	verbrennen
Burnout	ousgebrendt	ausgebrannt
Burst	geblatzt	zerplatzen
bush	shtohk	Busch
But	aber	aber
Butcher	metzel	Metzger
butt	stosen	zusemenstost
Butter	boodar	Butter
Butterfly	fleddermouse	Schmetterling
Button	knopf	Knopf
Buttonhole	knoploch	Knopfloch
Buy	ca fah	kaufen
Cabbage	graut	Kraut
Cackel	schnotera	gackern
cake	kuchen	Kuchen
calf	kalb	Kalb
Calf	kel vel	Kalb
Call animal	low kah	rufen
Call	roof	rufen
Camera	ab nemer	Kamera
Chamomile	cam mil ah	Kamille
Can you lift	poak sh du das	pazken
Can	kanne	Kann
Cancer	graps	Krebs

Candle	cartz	Kerze
Candy	canday	Bon bons
cane	shtock	Stock
Cap	cop	Mütze
Capsize	umgeschmissen	umgeworfen
Capture	fung	gefungen
card	carte	Karte
Care	fursorga	sorgen
Careful	boss oof	vorsichtig
Carpet	caraboda	Teppich
Carrots	gehl reba	Gelbe rube
Carry	drog gah	tragen
carve	ausschnide dah	ausshnieden
Casket	loh d	sarg
Casket	toten lahd	toten kiste
Caster	reddle	möbelrolle
Cat	katz	Katze
Catch	fonga	fangen
Catch	shnap f	einschnnappen
Caterpillar	raube	raupe
Cattle	rindfich	rinder
Celebrate	fy er ah	feieren
Cellar	keller	keller
Cemetery	carich hof	friedhof
Chain	kate	Katte
Chair	shtool	stuhl
Chapped	shroon ah	schrunde
Chase	nachfahra	jagen

Chase	yah kt	ver jagd
Chase	yawk	jagen
Chatter	bau bol	
Chatter	bob bah lah	schwatzen
Cheap	billich	billig
Cheat	moog lah	mogeln
Cheek	back ah	backe
Cheers wedding	yuke sah	
Cheese	kass	käse
Cherry	karsche	Kirsche
Chest	kishte	kiste
Chicken	hingle	huhn
Child	kind	kind
Children	kinder	kinder
Chill	freer	kalt
Chime	clocka	glockenspiel
Chimney	kom me ah	kamin
Chin	bord	.
Chintzy	geitsich	geizig
Choke	faarshticka	verschtycken
Christmas tree	weinachtsbaum	weihnachtsbaum
Chunks	broke ah	brocken
Church	carich	kirche
Churchyard	car ich hof	Kirchhof
Churn	butterfasssel	butterfass
Circle	gringle room	kreis
City	shtadt	stadt
Classy	gross ardich	gross ardich

Clatter	kleb ber ah	lärm
Clay	lah mah	ton
Clean (v.)	boots	putzen
Clean off	abbutze	abbutze
Clean	sauber machen	sauber machen
Clean	sow fahr	sauber
Climber	grawtler	kletterer
Clock	uhr	uhr
Close	mach zu	zu machen
Closet	schonk	schrank
Clot	broke ah	klumpen
Cloth	duch	tuch
Clothes line	vesh lyn	wäsche leine
Clothes	glah tar	Kleider
Cloud	volga	volke
Clown	sh pahr ah fontel	clown
Clubs	grites	kreuz
Cluck	glook	glucke
Clumsy	bot shich	tol palschig
Clumsy	ung sheekt	unge schickt
Coalmine	kohlagroaber	kohlenmiene
Coarse	grow eb	rauh
Coat	kittle	mantel
Coax (animals)	low ka	zureden
Coax (animals)	roof ah	rufen
Cob	kol bah	kolben
Cobbler	shumacher	schumacher
Cobweb	spinnenhoodle	spinnwebe

Coffee	coffay	kaffee
Coffin	dode lod	sarg
Cold	kalt	kalt
Collar	grawah	kragen
Collection box	kling el bite e	klingel beutel
Colt	voochel	fohlen
Comb	shtrel	kamm
Come here	kom da herr	kommen
Commotion	shpah dow kell	teumult
Commotion	shpay daawh kle	teumult
Complain	Broot lah	beshwerden
Confused	vas da dye hanker	verwirrt
Continually	alsfort	fortwährend
Conversation	maistube	gespräch
Convulsion	gahs ah gich ter	konvulsiv
Cook	koh hah	koch
Cookie	keech el	keks
Cool off	ab kichla	kuhl
Cool	keel	kühl
Copier	abschreiber	abschreiber
Copper	koopfer	kupfer
Cord	shnoor	kabel
Cork	sh top fahr	korken
Corn	velshkorn	mais
Corner stone	ek ston	eckstein
Cornice	granze	sims
Corpse	doteman	leich
Corsage	sh trise al	ansteckblume

Cottage cheese	shmear kase	hüttenkase
Cotton	vada	baumvolle
Cough	hoosh ta	husten
Cover	day gal	bedecken
Cover	deckal	decke
Cow	koo	kuh
Coward	hose ah shisser	feigling
Cox comb	ko vel	hahnenkamm
Crab	greps	krebs
crack	sh prung ah	sprung
Cracker	grackis	kracker
Cradle	vog	wiege
Crank	dragger	kurbel
Crawl	grah dell	krabbeln
Crayon	colour	stift
Crazy	farucht	ferrückt
Cream	rahm	sahne
Cricket	grick sel	grille
Critical	gridlich	kritisch
Crochet	haigla	häkeln
Crock	dopf	topf
Crooked	shray ges	schräg
Crooked	grume	krum
Cross	greitz	kreuz
Crossways	ebeers aches	quer
Crossways	ebeers aches	überkreuz
Crossways	eva tsvich	uberkreuz
Crow	grop	krähe

Crowbar	gleb eisen	brecheisen
Crumbs	groom lah	krümel
Crutch	gricke	krücke
Cry (quietly)	hyla	schreien
Cry	brilla	schreien
Cucumber	gah gume ar	gurke
Cuff	bry sell	stulpe
Cup	becher	becher
Cup	cape full	becher
Cupboard	shonk	schrank
Curious	wunderfitsich	neugierig
Curley	groos elich	lockig
Curls	groosla	locken
Currently	alleweil	Kürzlich
Curry horse	shtreeg lah	striegel
Curry comb	shtriggel	striegel
Curtain	forhang	vorhang
Cut	sh nide dah	schneidin
Cut	shnite	schneit
Damp	feicht	feucht
Dance	danz	tanz
Darn	flicka	stopfen
Darn	fah dolt lich	verdammten
Day	dag	tag
Dead	dodt	tot
Deaf	daub	taub
Dear	lee b	liebechen
Declare	glaw gah	klagen

deer	hirschecoo	reh
Devil	dife al	teufel
diagonally	iver ecks	diagonal
Diamond	eck shtahn	karo
Diaper	vindel	windel
Die	shtarba	gestorben
Difference	untersheet	unterschiedlich
Different	fersheedenez	verschieden
Dig	graba	graben
dig	grauva	grauben
Dim	donkel	dunkel
Dime	zehn	zehnerl
Dine	essen	essen
Dipper	shepf lefel	schöphlöffel
Dirt	dreck	dreck
Discharge	los gay	los lassen
Disengage	lows mache	freimachen
Dish rag	shpeel loomba	spüllumpen
Dish	shissel	schïssel
Dishes	g shar	geschir
Dissent	ab rode	abraten
Distribute	aus dell	aus teilen
Ditch	grauva	grauben
Dizzy	dar am lich	schwindlig
Dizzy	shvind lich	schwindlig
Do you	doosh	machst du
Doctor	doucter	artz
Dog	hund	hund

Doll	boob al	puppe
Doll	boop	puppe
Done	fartich	fertig
Donkey	aysel	asel
Door	dare	tur
Dot	dip fell	punkt
Dough	dag ich	teig
Dove	daube	taube
Doves	dow vah	tauben
Down There	droon ah	da unten
Down	knop	runter
Down	rowp	unter
Dowry	aus shteir	aussteuer
Dozen	dute zet	dutzend
Drag	shloff ah	ziehen
Drandruff	shee vah	schuppen
Draw	mol	malen
Drawer	shoop laud	schubladen
Draw-knife	schnitzmesser	schneidemesser
Dream	drah ma	traum
Dream	draum	traum
Dress	roke	kleid
Dresser	commode	kommode
Dried eye matter	motz	sandmännchen
Dried up	op gadree geld	abgetrokent
Drill	bohrea	bohren
Drink	sauf	trinken
Drink	zauf	zaufen

Drive	fah rah	fahren
Drop	dropfa	triofeb
Drown	versoufa	ertrinken
Drunk	roauch	rausch
Drunkard	loomp	trinker
Dry off	obdruckle	abdrickle
Dry	dar	dörr
Dry	drickle	trocken
Dry	druk ich	trocken
Duck	gutsch	ente
Dung fork	mistgabel	mistgabel
during	iver em	wahrend
Dust (off)	ab shtabah	abstauben
Dust	schtab	staub
dusty	sh tob ich	staubig
Dusty	shtaubich	staubig
Dwarf	groop fich	zweig
Dwarfed	motz sich	geschrumpft
Each time	yed es mol	yedes mal
Each	ah yade ar	jedes
Each	yeder	yeder
Eagerly	guy are lich	eifrig
Eagerness	I fur	begeirig
Ear lobe	ohra lepple	ohrläppchen
Ear	oar	ohr
Earring	Ohrahangela	ohring
Early	free ah	früh
easy	lie icht	leicht

Eat Seeds	geh neff far ah	
Eat	essa	essen
Eat	fress	fressen
Eaves drop	law are ya	lauchen
Edge	sh nap pah lah	rand
Effert	I fer	eiffer
Egg	eig	ei
Eggs	ieier	eier
Embrace	garnmacha	umarmen
empty	lehr	leer
Emptying	ausleeren	ausleren
Encircle	gringle room	umkreisen
Engrave	einsschneiden	gravieren
Enough	gah noonk	genug
Entangled	far hood elld	verstricken
Entire	gonz	ganz
Entrails	dar em	darm
Entrance	Eingang	eingang
Envelope	brief sak	umschlag
Erace	evec machen	löschen
Escape	durich gong ah	enkommen
Estimate	ob shates ah	einschätzen
Even	aye vaht	glatt
Evening	abend	abend
Evenings	ovetts	abenden
Ever	yeh mals	jemals
Ever	yeh	jemals
Everywhere	eva ral	überall

exaggerated	iv ah driv ah	übertreiben
Examine	besichtich	untersuchen
Exema	grind	ekzem
Exert	veyrik	anweden
Exerted	far yacht	anweden
Expensive	dyer	teuer
Experience	err lab bah	erfrahrung
Eye	aug	auge
Eye-glass	augenglas	brille
Face	gsicht	gesicht
Faded	ab geb schos ah	verblasseb
Fall	nah fal ah	fallen
Fall	shpode yahr	
Fall	st tart sah	sturzen
Farmer	foramahr	bauer
fart	fortsah	pfursen
Fashion	mode	mode
Fast	geschwind	schnell
Fat	fett	fett
Father-in-law	geh shvere	schwiegervater
Fatten	may sh tah	mästen
Fault	shulte	schulde
Fear	ungst	angst
Feast	fay sht	fest
Feather	fedder	feder
February	Fay bra vahr	Februar
Feed	feudar	foodahr
Feed	feudara	fütterm

Feel	sh peer	fühlen
Fellow	kah el	Kumpel
Felt boot	burga stiefel	filstiefel
Female	vibes bild	weibsbild
Fetch	hole ah	holen
Fiddle	geige	geige
Field	Feld	feld
Fierce	graw lich	grimnug
Fifteen	foch tsain	funfzehn
Fifty	fuf tsich	fümzig
Fight	sh trite	streit
Figs	fy ich ah	feige
Filth	sav ah rye	schmutzig
Finally	endlich	endlich
Find	fin ah	finden
Fine (legal)	blecha	blechen
Finger	fingah	finger
Finish	dah hawsh	beenden
Fire	fy ar	feuier
Firewood	brennholz	brennholz
First Communion	nacht mol	erstkommuion
First	erscht	erstens
Fist	fauscht	faust
Fits	bosst	passend
Fitted	gebaussed	anpassen
flag	fawn ah	fahne
Flail arms	fechtla	dreschflegel
Flame	flamme	flamme

Flannel	fin elle	flannell
Flask	flasche	flassche
Flatiron	beegle isa	bügeleisen
Flax	flox	flachs
Flies	meegah	fliegen
Float	schwinmen	schwimmen
Floor	boda	boden
Florist	blumengartner	florist
Flour	mehl	mehl
Flower	blooma	blume
Fly trap	miggafaggen	fliegenfalle
Fly	flieha	fliegen
Fly	mick	müche
Foam	shaum	schaum
Fool	norr	idiot
Foolishness	google furr	dummheit
Foot	foose	fuss
Foot-ball	fuseball	fussball
Force	gch valt	kraft
forehead	sh tarn	stirn
Forest	vald	wald
Forever	evig	ewig
Fork	gabel	gabel
Fork	gah vel	gabel
Forward	far shich	vorwärts
forward	farshicht	vorwä rts
Fountain	springbrunnen	quelle
Fowl	getziffer	ungezifer

Fox	foo ks	fuchs
Fox-chase	fuchs yaw gt	fuchs jagd
Frame	rhom	rahmen
Freeze	free rah	frieren
Frequently	all ay gebote	oft
Fried corn meal	ma ma licka	
Friend	fry end	freund
Fright	shrek ah	schreck
Frog	groat	frosch
From where	von woha	von
Frugal	sh pahr sum	spartanisch
Fruit core	boot sah	kern
Fruit	opes	obst
Fry	brot	braten
Frying pan	bratpfanne	pfanne
Fun	ge schpaws	spass
Fun	shpass	spass
Funeral	leicht	beeredingund
Funnel	dray ich tar	trichtar
Funny	geh spes ich	spassig
Furniture	mayvel	möbel
Furrow	furche	furche
Fussy	nide ich	widerspänstig
Gallop	galopp	gallop
Garlic	gno vel ich	knoblauch
Gate	tor	tur
Gather	fas lah	zusammenseihen
Gather	fessel	zusammenseihen

gather	tsoma geh macht	zusammen machen
Geese	gens	gänse
Genuflect	knee buege	knie beuge
Gertrude	got trout	Gertrude
Get	hol ah	holen
Get	greek	bekommen
Get	hole	bekommen
Get	holla	holen
Ghost	gascht	geist
Gift	gay shank	geschenk
Giggle	kitt eh rah	kichern
Girl	madel	madechen
Give	gebb	geben
Glass pane	shibe	scheibe
Glass	gloss	glas
Glasses	brilla	brille
Glassy	gläsich	glasig
Glove	handshing	handschuh
Go	gaya	gehen
Goat	gazabok	zeigen bock
Goblet	becher	becker
God Father	daf fot ar	pate
God Mother	daf gettle	patin
Going	gay ah	gehe
Gone	capute	veg sein
Good	gute	gut
Goodness	oi ee yo ee yoh	meine güte
Goodness	yea are mah licha	meine güte

Goose	gonz	gans
Gooseberries	groos el bera	staachelberre
Gossip	babbla	geschwätz
Gossip	retch	geschwatz
Got loose	los gungah	los gerissen
Grainery	gran ar	getreidespeincher
Grandmother	grossel	grossmutter
Grape	draub	traube
Grapes	drauba	traube
Grass	graws	gras
Grave yard	kar ich hof	friedhof
Grave	grab	grab
Gravestone	grabstein	grabstein
graze	vah dell ah	grasen
Grease	schmutz	fettig
Green	gree anh	grun
Greet	grusz	gruss
Grind sharpen	schleifa	scheiflen
Grind	mah la	mahlen
Grindstone	schleifstein	mahlstein
Groan	grakes	stöhnen
Ground feed	shroad	shrot
Ground	grund	grund
Guardian angel	schutzengel	schutzengel
Gun	flint	gewehr
Guzzle	sow fah	schlucken
Gypsy	zee gine ar	zigeuner
Had	hot cut	haben

Hail	shlow sah	hagel
Hair	whore	haar
Hairbrush	horbarsht	haarbürst
Hairpin	hornodel	haarnadel
Hairy	hor ich	haarig
Halter	halifter	halfter
Ham	shonnka	schinken
Hand	ha ond	hand
Handkerchief	nos dooch	taschen tuch
handle	shteel	griff
Handsaw	hondsag	handsäge
Handy	geh sicht	geschickt
Happened	baziert	passiert
Happy	fro	fröhlich
Hard	hort	hart
hare	hoss	hase
Harness	g shar	gescherr
Harrow	aye g	egge
Harvest	arn ah	dente
Hat	hoot	hut
Hatch	breedla	ausbruten
Hatchet	bile	beil
Hatching	breedla	brutend
haul	feerah	ziehen
haul	feerah	schleppen
Have (you)	haw sh	habben
Have	hawb	haust
Have	hush	haven

hawk	heenahvie	habicht
Hay stack	hi shtock	heuhaufen
Hay	hi	heu
Head cheese	shwart ah mogah	
Head	koepf shettle	kopf
Healthy	gesund	gesund
heap	haufen	haufen
Hearse	totewagen	leichenwagen
Heart	herz	herz
Heater	heitsofen	heizung
Heavy	shvare	schwer
Heel	absats	absatz
help	hilf	helfe
Hen	henne	henne
Here	doh hah	hier
Here	dough ah	hier
Herring	haring	hering
Hic up	glue k sir	schluckauf
Hidden	forshtaygelled	verstecht
Hide	fur shteckle	verstechen
High	ho uch	hoch
Hill	bar ick	berig
Hill	barr ig	berig
Hill	hoo vel	hügel
Hilly	buglig	hügelig
Hinge	baund	scharnier
Hip	hifp	hüfte
His	sine	sein

Hit	schlock	schlagen
Hitch up	ine span ah	einspannen
Hoe	hauck	hacke
Hog pen	saushtall	saustall
Hoist	ruf zeigen	hochziehen
Hold	hayva	halten
Hold	hebb	heb
Hole	loch	loch
Holiday	fire dog	feiertag
Holler	gry ish	schreier
Homely	hes lich	nicht hübsch
Homliest	veeshtist	hässlichste
Honeknife	schnitmesser	schleifmesser
Honest	ehrlich	ehrlich
Honey	hune ich	honig
Hop	hopsa	hüpfen
Horse small	raisel	Kleinpferd
Horse	pferd	pferd
Horse	rohs	pferd
Hot house	dreibhaus	glashaus
Hour-glass	stundenglas	stundenglas
Hunger	hong ahr	hunger
hunt	yecht lah	jagen
Hunter	yechtler	jäger
Hurry	ala ala	eilen
Hurt	bless eart	verletzt
Hurt	shmartsa	schmerz
Hushed	dush bar	still

Ice cream	gefrobrenes rahm	eis
Icecold	eiskalte	eiskalt
If	ven	wenn
Ill	kronk	krank
Impish	durich driv ah	durchtrieben
In a Circle	um gringel rum	in einem kreis
Indian	Indianer	Indianer
Indulgences	en fang an niss	frömen
Ink	dinda	tinte
Inkstand	dintenfass	dintenfass
Insignificant person	hose ah shisssser	unbedutcende mensch
Intelligent	geh shite	intelligent
Intense	veetich	intensiv
Intermittently	ali gehbot	manchmal
Interpreter	dol match shar	dolmetscher
Intestines	koo tel	eingeweide
Invite	einlauda	einladen
Iron	beeg lah	buglien
Iron	beegla	bügeleisen
Iron	isa	eisen
Iron	ise ah	eisen
Is	ish	ist
It appears	ver sheinlich	wahrscheinlich
It hurts	oh vay	es schmerzt
Jacket	mondle	mantel
January	Yona vahr	Januar
Jar	bonga	glass
Jew	yute	jude

Jovial	Lushtig	lustig
Joy	frah d	freude
Judge	free dens richter	richter
Jug	grug	krug
Juice	bree ah	saft
July	Yew lee	Juli
Jump	hopes	hüpfen
Juneberry	yuna bera	juni Berri
June	you knee	Juni
Junk	tzikes	zeug
Kernel	gutsla	kern
Kettle	kay sell	kessel
Key	schlee sel	schlüssel
Key-hole	schllussselloch	schlüssellock
Kick	ausschlauga	schlag
Kick	dret da	treten
Kick	sh trom fla	strampelen
Killed	umgebrunga	umbrungen
Kind	leevus	lieb
King	kannich	könig
Kiss	schmitzel	kuss
Kitchen	keech	kuche
Knee	ken eeah	knie
Kneel	knieen	knien
Knife	messar	messer
Knit	shtreeka	stricken
Knock	glopf	klopfen
Knot	g noo bah	knöph

Knot	knephf el	knoten
Knotted	vergnoobeld	geknöpht
Know	voss	wissen
Kool aid	flavor vasser	
Label	zettel	zettel
Laborer	gnecht	knecht
Lace peaks	tsocka	speitze
Lace	spitza	speitze
Lad	booha	junge
Ladle	shepf lefel	schöpfer
Lady	fra	frau
Lamb	shaifel	lamm
Lame	lah m	lahm
Lamp	licht	lampe
Land	lond	land
language	sh proche	sprache
lantern	lah darn	laterne
Lard	schmootz	schmalz
Last year	for rahm yohr	voriges jahr
Last	let sht	letztens
Late	sh pode	spät
Laugh	lach	lachen
Laughter	lah eh ha	das Lachen
Laundry	veshas	die Wäsche
Lawyer	affe gaht	anwalt
Lawyer	freedens richter	rechtsgelehrtele
laxative	lox ear	abführend
Lay	lay yah	legen

Lazy	faul	faul
Lazy	litterich	liederlich
Lead pencil	"bleishrift, bleisvise"	bleistift
Leaf	blatt	blatt
Leak	rinn	Rinnen
Leaking	rint	leck
Lean	mah gahr	mager
Leap	springen	springen
Learn	lahr ah	lernen
Left	lynx	links
Leg	shenkle	bein
Leggy	shenglish	lang beinig
Lemon	limone	zitrone
Lemonade	lemona vasser	limonade
length	long	länge
Let lay	liegen lossen	leigen lassen
Let	loss	loss
Letter	brief	brief
Letter	boo shtaw bah	Buchstabe
Lettuce	salat	salat
lick	shleck	lecken
Licorice	bar ah drek	bärendreck
Lid	deckel	deckel
Lie	lig yah	lüge
Life	lebe	leben
Light	licht	leicht
Lightening	blitz	blitz
Lightning rod	blitz ob liter	bleitzableiter

Like	gleich	gleich
Limp	geh gnop	hinken
Limping	kn ah bah	hinken
Lion	Loebe	löwe
Lip	lib el	lippe
Lips	lipple	lippen
liquor	schnapps	schnaps
Listen	haw rich	hören
Little calf	kel vel ah	kalb
Little flower	blee mal	Blümlein
Living room	fader stube	Wohnzimmer
Living space	shtoop	Lebensraum
Lizard	grotlar	Eidechse
Load	lauda	ladung
Loaf	lob	Leib
Lock	shlees	schloss
Lock	shlose	abschlienssen
Log	clotz	holzklotz
Look	loo yah	schauen
Look	looga	schauen
Look into	googla	untersuchen
Look	shauah	schauen
Loose	low bar	lose
Lop ear	lop ahr	
Lots	tsimlich	viel
Low	need ah	nieder
Lower	needa	nieder

Luggage	satchel	gepäck
Lukewarm	ubershlagen	lauwarm
Lumber yard	bauholz hof	holzplatz
Lumber	bauholz	holz
Lump	bolla	klumpen
Lumps	broga	klumpen
Mad	veedich	wütend
Magnifying glass	grosmacher glas	lupe
Mail bag	bosht sach	brieftasche
Mail	bosht	post
Make space	raum macha	platz machen
Male	mons kal	maunnlich
Man	mann	mann
Manger	gripf	krippe
Mannered	brof	brav
Manure	mischt	mist
Map	lancart	landkarte
Marble	mor a bul	marmor
March	Martz	Marz
Mare	shtoode	stute
Marriage	hochzeit	hochzeit
Married	fah hy ar rod	verheiratet
Mason	baurer	freimaurer
Match	fireholz	zündholz
Mattress	matratz	matratze
May	My	Mai
Maybe	ament	vielleicht
Maybe	fehr leisht	vielleicht

Mean	bays	gemein
Mean	veeshtol	Ungezogenheit
Measles	dray dla	masern
Meat	flah sh	fleisch
Medal	pfenning	medallie
Melon	melone	melone
Melons	bashtant	bestand
Men	menner	männer
Merely	blos	nur
Merriment	yuk sah	fröhlichkeit
Mess up	far batched	verpatzen
Mess	saw vah rye	verpatzt
Message	botshaft	nachricht
Mice	mise	mäuse
Middle	meed lah	mitte
Milk	mil ich	milch
Milk-can	milchcanne	milch kanne
Millet	meelat	Hirse
Mimic	shpatel	immitienran
Mind	sinn	sinn
Mirror	spiegel	spiegel
Miser	Kah rich	geizhals
Misplace	ferlege	verlegt
Mistake	feller	fehler
Mitten	handshing	handschuhe
Mix	far mishbull ah	rühren
Mix	mish bla	vermischen
Moan	yammer	jammern

Mock	sh pate la	verspotten
Moist	fy icht	feucht
Mold	groats ich	schimmel
Money	geld	geld
Monkey	off	affe
Month	monat	monat
Mooly	hornless cow	
Moon	mah	mond
Mornings	mariatz	morgen
Mosquito	shnoge	mosquita
Most	men sht	meiste
Mother in law	shveeger muter	schwiegermutter
Mouldy	groed sich	schimmelig
Mountain	barrick	berg
mourn	trauern	trauern
Mouse hole	mauseloch	mauseloch
Mouse	maus	maus
Mouth (slang)	gosh	
Much	aurich	viel
Much	feehl	viel
Muddy	schlimerich	schlammig
Mug	becher	becher
Mule	essel	esel
Mushroom	schwammah	pilz
Musician	shpeelman	muskar
Muskrat	mooshrat	maskerade
Must	moosh	muss
Mustard	saneft	senft

Mustach	sh now tsell	schnurbart
My goodness	eye eye eye	oi oi oi
Nag	gnunx	nörgeln
Nagging	grid lich	übertreiben
Nail	fingernagel	fingernagel
Nail	nogel	nagel
Naked	foo sell nack ich	guns nacht
Naked	naugich	nacht
Name	nom ah	name
Namesday	nom est dog	namens tag
Napkin	mauldoche	serviette
Naughty	baese	böse
Naughty	boesevichtig	bosheil
Naughtyness	boes hatt	basheil
Navel	nah vel	nabel
Near	neh vahr	nahe
Near	node	nahe
Nearer	nay yah	näher
Neck	geh nick	hals
Necklace	grella	halskette
Necktie	shloof	karwatte
Need	brauch	brauche
Needle	nodel	nadel
Needy	nay dich	bedürftig
Nephew	bruder sohn	neffe
Nest	nesht	nest
Never	niemals	nie
New	nye	neu

Newsboy	tzeitungs boo ah	zeitungsjunge
Next time	nay sht es mol	nächstes mal
Next to	navah	neben
Nice	sh ann	schön
nickname	iver nomah	spitzname
No	nah	nein
Nod (agree)	moog ah	nicken
Noise	bolla rah	lärm
Noise	lep dog	lärm
Noise	shpay dog el	lärm
Non sense	goo gal foor	unsinn
Nose	noss	nase
Nostril	nah sah looch	nosenloch
Not again	nee me	nicht mehr
Not	nit	nicht
Not	gar nit	nicht
Nothing	garn nix	nichts
November	No vember	November
Now a days	heit igsd dags	heutzutage
Now	alle vile	lürzlich
Now	yet zt	jetzt
Nowhere	narjeds	niergendwo
Number	shtrifah	nummer
Number	ziffer	nummer
Nun	schvester	nonne
Nut	gud sel	nuss
Nut	nuz	nuss

Oats	hovar	hafer
Occasionally	alle mol	manchmal
Ocean	meer	meer
October	October	Oktober
Odor	luder	geruch
Offered	ongedrawga	anbieten
Oh her	yoh dee ah	ach die
Oil	ail	öl
Oil-can	aylkann	öldose
Oil-well	aylbrunna	ölbrunnen
Ointment	sol ab	salbe
On purpose	tsu lodd	mit obsicht
On target	gah dro fah	getroffen
On the edge	shneb bah lah	auf der ecke
On top	droof	auf
On top	o vah	daraif
Once in a while	allay geh bote	manchmal
Once	amol	einmal
One	ani	eins
Onion top	shloot	zwiebel stiel
Onion	zvivel	zwiebel
Only	bloz	nur
Only	nurnoomal	einzigst
Open	oof	offen
Orange	boomeranz	orange
Organ	origle	orgel
Organ	foosargel	fussorgel

Orphan	stieve kind	waise
Other	aneras	anddere
Our	unser ah	unsere
Out	naus	aus
Out	rouse	heraus
Outhouse	beckhouse	kelhaus
Outside	drowez	draussen
Over seer	iber san her	aufpazser
Over	dreever	drüben
Over	droo vah	drüben
Over	iv ver	drüben
Overcoat	kittle	mantel
Overshoe	evershoog	überzichschuh
Overthere	driva	uber
overtired	meed	müde
Owl	ile	Eule
Own	I ah	eigen
Own	I gan ah	eigen
Pacifier	memmel	schnuller
Page	blatt	blatt
Paid	betsalt	bezahlt
Pail	aarmer	eimer
Paint brush	benzel	pinsel
Paint	fareb	farbe
Paint	on striche	anstreichen
Painter	onstreicher	anstreicher
Palms	balma	palmen
Pan	pfanne	pfanne

Pane (window)	scheibe	rahmen
Pant pooper	hose ah shisser	hosenscheissser
Panties	bloomars	unterhose
Pants	hose ah	hosen
Paper	babbeer	papier
Paper	zeitung	zeitung
Pare	schalen	schälen
Parents	eld der ah	eltern
Parlor	shtoup	stube
Parrot	bapagei	papergei
Past time	far whil e ah	verweilen
Past	far by	varben
Paste	bappes	kleber
Pat	ded shell	streichlen
Pay	betzall	bezahlen
Peace	frid ah	frieden
Peacock	boahanna	phau
Peach	pfarsheng	pfirsch
Peak	spitsa	spitze
Peanut	boonatz	erdnuss
Pear	beer	bier
Pears	beera	biere
Peek	geegla	gucken
Peeking	gigla	gucken
Peel	shay lah	schälen
Peep	geegla	gucken
Pen	feder	füller
Pencil	blivise	bleistift

Penny	zent	pfennig
People	lite	leute
Pepper	pfeffer	pfeffer
Perform marriage	drowe ah	trauung
Perhaps	ver shine lich	wahrscheinlich
Permission	darafa	erlaubnis
Person	Mench	Mensch
Pester	blohg	nerven
Pester	gah vale ah	kwälen
Pester	hecht la	feinde machen
Pester (to hurt)	hootsel	hunzen
Photo (take)	ab nemah	foto
Pick out	rouse lassah	auslesen
Pickax	beegle	hacke
Picky	grid lich	übertreiben
Picky eating	schlekerich	wählerisch
Picture	bild	bild
Piece	shtich	stück
Pig	sow	schwein
Pigeon	daube	taube
Piglets	sylala	ferkel
Pike	hecht	hecht
Pile	how fah	haufen
Piles	hi fah	heifen
Pill	bille	pille
Pillow	kissah	kissen
Pillow case	kissah tseechl	überzug
Pillows	kissen	kissen

Pinch	fetz	zwicken
Pipe	pfeife	pfeife
Pitcher	bitcher	krug
Pitchfork	gabel	mist gabel
Pitty	shaw da	schande
Pius	from	fromm
Place	blotz	platz
Planted	gepflantsa	planzen
Plant	pflansah	pflanze
Plate	dell ah	teller
Play	shpeel ah	spielen
Playmate	comaradle	kamerad
Plow	pfllug	pflug
Plum	pflaum	pflaume
Point	sh pits ah	spitze
Poison	gift	gift
Poker	durichmacher	feverhaken
pole	sh tong	stange
Polish	vixa	polern
Poop	shise	scheisse
Poor	arem	arm
Pope	babscht	papst
Poplar	bappel	pappel
Porcelain	barts lean	porzellan
Porch	forehaus	veranda
Portrait	bild	bild
Post	pfoshta	pfosten

Postman	brieftrager	briefträger
Postmark	postzeichen	poststempel
Pot	dopf	topf
Potato pancakes	grumbeerekiechle	kartofelkiechel
Potatoes	groom bera	kartofeln
Potty	heffel	haferl
Poultry	gestiefer	geflügel
Pour	shank	einscheken
Pour	sheet	giesen
Pour	shit	schütten
Pout	drootz	schmollen
Pray	bet	beten
Pray	bett ah	beten
Prayer	gebett	gebet
Preach	bray dichen	predigt
Preserves	ine gay macht	ein kochen
Press	drick	drüken
Prettiest	shoenshtest	schönste
Pretty	shan	schöen
Prevent	ob halten	ab halten
prick	shtech ah	stechen
Print	drook	drucken
Print	druuga	drucken
Prison	ieganfunes	gefängnis
Prisoner	eingaafangener	gefangener
Probably	wahscheinllich	vielleicht
Prompt	geh shvindt	gleich
Prompt	gly ich	schnell

Proud	schtolz	stolz
Prune	gvetch	pflaume
Prunes	gvetscha	pflaumen
Pug	groll	knoten
Pull	tseeg	ziehen
Pump	boomp	pumpe
Pumpkin	car eps	kürbis
Punch	loch eisa	schlag
Pup	yunger hund	welpe
Purse	gelt sock	gelvbeutel
Push	dricka	drücken
Push	sh toe sah	stossen
Pushed	gedrickt	gedrückt
put	sh tay lah	stellen
Putrid	luder	faul
Putrid	egglich	faul
Putty	gehgledt	kitt
Quarrelsome	sh tri dich	streitiusig
Queen	dahm	königin
Quick	schnell	schnell
Quickly	geh shwindt	schnell
quilt	sh pett el deck	quilt
Rabbit	haas	hase
Race horse	shpring rose	rennpferd
Radish	rettich	rettich
Rag	loom bah	lappen
Railroad	bahn	eisenbahn
Rainbow	regenboga	regebbogen

Rain-gauge	regenmess	regenmesser
Raise	oufmachen	in die höhe heben
Rake	rech el	rechen
Rake	recha	rechen
Raking	rechla	rechen
Rat	rotmouse	ratte
Rattle	geh clepper	rassel
Razor	razeermesser	rasierer
Reach	langa	reucgeb
Read	less ah	lesen
Reading	lessa	liest
ready	ein richt	fertig
Really	vichtig	wierklich
Recently	alle vile	kürzlich
Recollect	besinnen	sich besinnen
Rectum	off tar	Mastdarm
Red	rhod	rot
Reflect	beh rye ah	überlegen
Regret	kie ah	bereuen
Regret	lah d	Bedauren
Reindeer	hushkoo	rentier
Remember	gah denk	erinnern
Remember	im sinn halta	rentier
Reside	vohn	wohnen
Rest	ruha	ruhe
Rhubarb	pie shtangle	rhabarber
Rib	ribba	rippe
Ribbon	bendel	schürze

Ribbon	slipful	schleife
Ride	ridah	reiten
Rider	reiter	reiter
Right	recht	recht
Rind	schwarte	schwarte
Rip	schlitz	riss
Rip	shlentzer	riss
rock	sh tawn	stein
Roll	kal veh rah	rollen
Rolling pin	noodleholz	nuddle holz
Romp	day vah	tollen
Roof	dauch	dach
Roofs	dachah	dächer
Rooster	goghlar	hahn
Rooster	hanah	gockel
Root	vortzel	würzel
Rope ladder	strickladder	strickleiter
Rope	shtrick	stric
Rose hips	ash kitssela	
Rough	rowe ich	nicht glatt
Rub	rie bah	reiben
Rub	yuche	reiben
Rubbers	rowbershtiffle	überschuh
Ruckus	commody	krach
Rug	carapboda	teppich
Ruler	mess	linel
Run	shpring	laufen
Running	shpringa	rennen

Sad	betreebt	traurig
Sad	drawrich	traurig
Sad	dreeb	traurig
Saddle	sattel	sattel
Salamander	gratlar	salamander
Salt shaker	salz bick sel	salzdose
Salt	saltz	saltz
Sang	geh sungen	singen
Sass	maul ah (go sha)	Spott
Satiated	sot	satt
Saucer	blettel	undertasse
Save	sh par	sparen
Saw	sag	sägen
Scald	bree ah	skalde
Scale	vogue	waage
Scarcely	kah m	kaum
Scare	shrake ah	erschrecken
Scare	shrek	erschrecken
Scarecrow	fogelferdriver	vogelucheuche
Scared	fehr gel start	erschrecken
Scarf	shar ef	schaal
School teacher	schulmeister	lehrer
School	schule	schule
Scissors	schare	schere
Scold	shel dah	schimpfen
Scrape	shah vah	schaben
Scraps	sh pat la	reststücken
Scratch	grautza	kratzen

Screw driver	schraubezeiger	schraubenziecher
Screw	schraube	schraube
Scrub bush	Hay kah	strauch
Scythe	sense	sense
Sea	mare	meer
Seamstress	naggera	näherin
Searching	sooch hun	untersuchen
Seashells	meershallah	muschel
Seed	soma	samen
Seldom	venich	selten
Self	sel ver	selber
Selfish	misvergunstlich	selbstsüchtig
Send her	shick sah	schicken
Send	shick	schicken
Sent	geschicht	geschicht
September	Sayp tember	September
Serve	deinst	bedienen
Served	Ein geh shenkt	bedienen
Settle	aus mach ah	begleichen
Several	ett lich	etliche
sew machine	sh tepp machine	nähmachine
Sew	nag	nähen
Sew	nag ah	nähen
Shade	shedda	schatten
Shake	shit lah	schütteln
Shake	shittel	schütteln
Shame	shandlich	schande
Shame	shawned\	beschämen

sharp	sh pits ich	scharf
Sharpen	schlife ah	schleifen
Shave	raw see rah	resieren
Shawl	halsdouch	halstuch
Sheep	schohf	schafe
Sheepshearing	schaffscheren	schafe scheren
Sheet	line douch	tuch
Shells (shot gun)	boat ah rahn ah	patrone
Shiny	glitzeerich	glänzend
Shirt	hemp	hemd
Shit	shise	scheissen
Shoe	shoog	schuh
Shoe	shtiffel	schuh
Shoeblack	shtiffel vix	schuhwichse
Shoemaker	schumacher	schuhmacher
Shoot	shees sah	schiessen
Shop	ine cof ah	einkaufen
Short	cartz	kurz
Shot gun	shrode flint	schrotflinte
Should	soat	sollte
Should	soll sht	sollte
Shoulder	auk sol	schulter
Shout	greisha	schreien
Shovel	schaufel	schaufeln
Show	tsy ah	zeigen
Shrunk	ine gong ah	eingehen
Shut	tsu macha	zumachen
Shy	blade	scheu

Siblings	gshwishter	geschwesten
Sick	krank	krank
Sideway	neh vets	seitlich
Sigh	sife ar	seufzen
Signify	bay dites	bedeuten
Silk	side ah	Seide
Since	tsitter	seit
Sing	singa	Singen
Singe	sengle	sengen
single	let ich	ledig
Sister-in-law	geh shviere	schwägerin
Sit	hook	sitzen
Sit	hooka	sitzen
Skate	shly meh rah	schlittschuh laufen
Skull	harn sheddle	Schädel
skunk	sh tink cuts	Stinktier
Slant	shr aig	schräg
Slap	bot sh	schlagen
Slay	toten	töten
Sled	shliddila	Schlitten
Sleep	schlof	schlafen
Sleep	shlo fah	schlafen
Sleeve	ar em al	Armel
Sleigh	schlitta	schlitten
Sleighing	schlidas	schlitten fahren
Slimy	gleverich	schleimig
Sliver	shlifeer	schiefer

Slobber	lab beh rah	sabber
Slow	longsom	langsam
Sly	lish dich	listig
Small amount	bissel	klein beigeben
Small Bottle	flesch el	Fläschchen
Small child	menchel	Kleinkind
Small mouth	gay shel	kleiner Mund
Small	gla hn	klein
Small	glanner	kleiner
Smart	gscheit	klug
Smash	fermalen	zermahlen
Smell	schmach	riechen
Smile	sh mol ah	lächeln
Smoke	racha	rauchen
Smoker	raucher	Raucher
Smooth	glott	glatt
Snake	schlange	Schlange
Snap	sh nepf	schnappen
Snarl	shmur ah	knurren
Snoop	shmaus ah	schnüffeln
Snoop	shno fla	schnüffeln
Snot	roots	Rotz
Snout	rissel	rüsssel
Snow bank	schnee schonsa	Schneewehe
Snow	schnee	Schnee
Snowball	schnayballa	Schneeball
Snowman	schnayman	Schneeman
So there	dah hosh	da hast du es

So	drum	darum
Soak	ine wach ah	einweichen
Soaking wet	botch noss	durch nassen
Soap	soff	Seife
Sober	nichter	Nüchtern
Socialize	umgeben	sich umgeben
Sock	soh ka	Socke
Soft	vah ich	weich
Soldier	soldat	Soldat
Some one (male)	on are	jemand
Some	etwas	etwas
Some	mon ich ah	maniche
Someone female	on ee	eine
Someone	ebbar	jemand
Somersault	bartsel boak	Purzelbaum
Something	ebbs	etwas
Sometimes	mon ich mol	manchmal
Sometimes	alle mohl	manchmal
Somewhat	etwas	etwas
Somewhat	zimmlich	zeimlich
somewhere	arietz	irgendwo
somewhere	eerie gan voo	irgendwo
Son in law	dock ter mann	Schwiegersohn
Song	leed	Lied
Soon	bal	bald
Soon	gleich	gleich
Sophisticated	gross ardich	gebildet
Sort	sah vote	Sorte

Soul	sele	Seele
Soup	soop	Supe
Sow	einschlagen	Säen
Sow	los	Sau
Spade	sh owe ful	Spaten
Spades	sheeba	Schippen
Spank	how ah	hauen
Sparce	vanich	wenig
sparrow	spatz	spatz
Spectacles	brilla	Brille
Speculate	ts fife al	zweifeln
Spice	Kvartz	Gewurtz
Spider web	sh pin ah hoodle	Spinnennetz
Spider	sh pin	Spinne
Spike	groser nagel	Langer Nagel
Spill	ferschutten	verschütten
Spill	shvov lah	verschüttenes
Spills	geh shwabble	verschüttenes
Spirited	loosh dich	lüstig
Spit	sh bowt	spuken
Spitoon	shpauch becher	Spucknapf
Splash	lep per ah	Spritzen
splinter	sh prize ar	Splitter
Split	shpalt ah	spalten
Spool	rettle	Spule
Spoon	lefel	Löffel
Spot	fleck ah	Flecken
Sprained	ver enged	verstauchen

Spring	gvell, free yohr	Quelle
sprinkle	sh prenz	sprenkeln
Sprinkler	geese kan	Giesskanne
Square	echig	Viereckig
Square	fingel	Quadratmass
Squeezed	getricht	drücken
squirt	sh pritz	spritzen
Stab	shtoofa	erstechen
Stacked	gezetzt	stapeln
Stairs	shtawfel	Treppe
Stallion	hengsht	Hengst
stamper	sh tem fel	Stampfer
stand	shtay ah	stehen
Star	starna	Stern
Start	on fonga	anfang
Startled	shrages	erschrencken
Stay Out	blibe drous	draussen bleiben
Stay	blipe	bleiben
Steal	gvitch	stehlen
steal	shteh lah	stehlen
Steam	dammpf	Dämpf
Steam	dunsht	Dunst
Steamed	fer dempft	verdampfen
Steer	stiera	steuern
step mother	sh teef mutter	Stiefmutter
step	sh tau ful	Stufe
Step	shrit	Schritt
Stick	bengel	Stock

Stick	sh tecca	Stock
Sticky	bebich	klebrig
stiff	sh tife	steiff
Still yet	noch	noch
Still	als noch	noch
Still	roo ich	rühig
stitch	sh tich	stich
Stocking cap	tsiffel cop	Zipfelmütze
Stocking	shtroomph	Strumpf
Stolen	geh shtola	verstohlen
Stomach	baugh	Bauch
Stomach	mah gah	Magen
Stone	stein	Stein
Stool	shtuhl	Stuhl
Stop	hair oof	halten
Stop	hope	halten
Storm	shturm	Sturm
Stove	offa	Ofen
Straight	cart zeh grod	gerade
Straight	grod	gerade
Strain	sigh ah	abseihen
Strainer	sigh are	Seiher
Strange	fremd	fremd
Strange	on feld ich	einfältig
Stranger	fremder	Fremder
Straw	helma	Halm
Straw sack	sh tro sock	Strohsack
Straw	hel ma	Stroh

Street	shtreet	Strasse
Stretch	sh treg ah	strecken
Strike	shlagga	schlagen
String	schnur	Schnur
Stripes	sh trah fell ah	Streifen
Strong	shtau rick	Stark
Stud	hengsht	Hengst
Students	scheeler	Schüler
stuff	sache	Sachen
stuff	shtope fah	Stoff
Stuff	tsike	Seug
Stuff	gsheft	zeichs
stumble	shtol bar ah	stolpern
Stump	stumpf	Stumpf
stupid	sh teef al	dumm
Such	so viah	so wie
Suffer	mit lita	leiden
Sugar	tsoogar	Zucker
Sulphur	shve vel	Schwefel
Summersault	bar tsel book	purzelbaum
Sun	sonne	Sonne
Sunday	soon dog	Sonntag
Sunflower	carna	Sonnenblumen
Sunrise	sunoofgangen	Sonnenaufgang
Sunset	sunopgeht	Sonnenuntergang
Suppose	verschienlich	wahrscheinlich
Surprise	eye yie yah	überraschung
Suspect	ts vife ful	verdächtiger

Sustain self	nair ung	aufrechterhalten
Swallow	shloo ga	schlucken
Swallow	shveh veh la	schwalbe
Swear	floo cha	fluchen
Sweat	shvitz	schwitzen
Sweep	fag	fegen
Sweep	fagga	fegen
Sweet	sees	süss
Swim	schwim	schwimmen
Swine	schwein	Schwein
Swing	gong sh	Schaukel
Swing	shlenk ar ah	schaukeln
Swollen	geh shvollen	geschwollen
Table spoon	es lafel	Esslöffel
Table	disch	Tisch
Tag	zettel	Zettel
Tail	vah doll	Schwanz
Tail	shvanz	Schwanz
Take	nem ah	nehm eh
Take Over	ivver nemah	übernehmen
Take	nem ah	nehmen
Take	nemm	nehmen
Tale	rayt sell	Erzählung
Tamp	shto sah	stosse
Tamp	shtum phas	stophmasse
Tangled	farhoodled	versticken
Tangled	vergehnoobled	verwicklung
Tank	tank	Behälter

Tape measure	mess	Massband
Tassel	draw sell	Drowssel
Tassel	tsawsel	Drowssel
Taste	farsucht	versuchen
Tattered	mar eb	zerlumpt
Tavern	saufas platz	Kneipe
Tea	taya	Tee
Teacher	deetchera	Lehrer
Teacup	tea kepfel	Teetasse
Teapot	teakanne	Teekanne
Tear	ferreisa	zerreissen
Tease	arageren	ärgern
Teaspoon	kline laffel	Teelöffel
Teats	dittel	zitze
Teeth	zahne	Zähne
Terrible	shrake lich	schreklich
Thaw	losch	schmelzen
Then	no dart	danach
Then	node	dann
Then	noder	dann
There	dart	da
Therefore	dar rum	darum
These	dena	disse
They are	see sont	sie sind
Thick	dick	dick
Thief	dieb	Dieb
Thief	sh pits boo	Dieb
Thimble	finger hoot	Fingerhut

Thin	dunn	dünn
Thin	maugar	mager
Thirst	darscht	durst
Thistles	hexa	Distel
Thought	gadenkt	Gedanke
Thread	netz	Zwirn
Thread	schnur	Schnur
Threshold	shvell ah	Shwelle
Through	durich	durch
Throw	schmisa	werfen
Throw	shmise	werfen
Thumb	dauma	Daumen
Thunder	doomela	Donner
Thursday	duners dog	Donnerstag
Tick	zeck	Zecke
Ticket	dicket	Eintritskarte
Tickle	keetzla	keetzeln
Tidy up	ooff rauma	oufräumen
Tie	binden	binden
Tie	schnoor	Krawatte
Tie	shloopf	fest
Tight	fay sht	fest
Time	tzite	Zeit
Tingle	fingle	kribbeln
Tiny	grupfich	winzig
Tired	bad	müde

Tired	meed	müde
To bloom	blig ah	blühen
To Love	leevah	lieben
To morrow	mar ee yah	morgen
Tongue	tsung	zunge
To roll	kah rich lah	rollen
To saw	sag ga	sägan
To say	saw gah	sägen
To spite	tsu lod	boesheit
Tobacco	doovak	Tabak
Today	hite	Heute
Toe	tsay ah	Zehe
Together	tsusomma	Zusammen
Tomato	bara dise affel	Tomate
Tombstone	grabstein	Grabstein
Tomorrow	mar ee yah	Morgen
Toothpick	zahnsteck	Zahnstocker
Top	dure donser	kreisel
Top	ovah	Spitze
Torment	blo ah	quälen
Torn	verisa	zerrissen
Torture	hootz la	qual
Toss	schmise	werfen
Towel	handduch	Handtuch
Town	shtadt	Stadt
Toys	spielzige	Spielzeug
Track	sh poor	Spur
Tramp on	droppa	trampeln

Trap	falle	Falle
Tree	baum	baum
Triangle	drei eckich	Dreieck
Trot	drabba	trotten
Troubles himself	gvaled sich	sich quälen
Trough	drog	Trog
Truck	drok	Lastwagen
Trunk	keesht	Kiste
Trust	drowe ah	vertrauen
Tub	vesk kee vil	washkübel
Tube	rohrel	Röhre
Tuesday	dinsh dog	Dienstag
Tumble	bartz el	purzeln
Turkey	velsh hanna	Trutahn
Turn	drag	umdrehen
Turtle	shilgroat	Schildkröte
Twig	zweig	Zweig
Typewriter	schreibmaschine	Schreibmaschine
Ugly	hesslich	hässlich
Umberella	shirem	Regenschirm
Un hitch	aus spann ah	ausspannen
uncalm	fit sich	unruhig
Under wing	hooder	unter den flügel
Under	oon ar	unter
Underwear	under hosa	Unterhemd
Undressed	aus geh tsogen	ausziehen
Unhappy	betreebt	betrubt
Universal	geh mine shoft	allgemein

Unless	shoen sht	ansonst
Unload	opladen	abladen
Unlock	oopfschlliesen	aufschliessen
Unnecessary	oonaitich	unnötig
Unneeded	unnadeich	unnotig
Unpack	ouspaken	auspacken
Untie	los binah	los binden
Up there	droh vah	do oben
Up	dro vah	rauf
Up	noof	obenauf
Up	ovah noof	oben
Uphere	hoe vah	oben
Upon	oof	auf
Urban dweller	shtetler	Stadtmensch
Vaccinate	impfah	impfen
Valise	manteldraug	Mantelsack
Valley	deefing	Tal
Various	verschiedenes	verschieden
Varnish	law k	Lack
Vegetables	garta soch	Gemüse
Veil	shly ahr	Shaal
Velvet	saw mitt	Samt
Vest	brushduch	Unterhemd
Vestibule	furhaus	Vorhaus
Vicinity	geh end	umgebung
Village	shtett al	Dorf
Violet	veilchen	Violett
Violin	gike	Geige

Vomit	coats	Kotzen
Wabbly	loberich	wacheln
Wagon	vah ga	Wagen
Wait	vart	warten
Walk off	ab laffa	abgenutzt
Walk	la fah	laufen
Wall	vandt	wand
Waltz	valtz	Waltzer
Want	wilt	wollen
Was	geh vest	gewesen
Wash	weshah	waschen
Washboard	veshbret	Waschbrett
Washing	vesha	waschen
Wasteful	shaad	schade
Water	vasser	Wasser
Way	veg	Weg
We	mir	wir
Weak	mareb	schwach
Wedding	hochtsig	Hochzeit
Wednesday	mit voch	Mittwoch
Weeds	ungraut	Unkraut
Week	woch	Woche
Weep	hile lah	Heulen
Weigh	veega	wiegen
Weld	shvess ah	schweissen
Well	Bruna	Brunnen
Well	vas ich	na ja
Wet	noss	nass

Wheat	frucht	Weizen
Wheat	vatsah	Weizen
Wheel barrow	shoop car ich	Schubkarren
Wheel	rot	Rad
When	ven ay ah	wenn
Where	woha	wo
Whether	abe	ob
Whey	molkah	Molke
Whine	geh nung sah	winseln
Whip	bytsh	Peitschen
Whiskey	shnaps	Schnaps
Whisper	bish per ah	flüstern
White horse	shim mel	Schimmel
White	vice	weiss
Whitewasher	onstreiker	tünche
Whittle	schnitzel	schnitzen
Who	var	wer
Whom	vem	wem
Whore	hoor	Hure
Why	vah room	warum
Wide	braad	breit
Wiggly	tzittrich	zittrig
Will be	vart	zufallig
With	mitt	mit
Window curtin	for hongl	vorhang
Window pane	shibe	fenster Scheibe
Window	feng ster	Fenster
Window	sheiva	Fenster

Wing	fleegel	Flügel
Wipe	boots	putzen
Wipe	ab visha	abwischen
Wipe	abbutz	abputzen
Wipe	ahb ge wisha	abputzen
Wipe	butz	putzen
Wire	droad	draht
With	mit	mit
Without	ooh na	ohne
Wolf	volef	Wolf
Woman	waibsbild	frau
Women	veiver	Frauen
Wood	holz	Holz
Work	shoffa	Arbeiten
Work (labor)	aus shauf ah	Arbeiten
Worked	geh shoft	ge arbeitet
Worm	wahrum	wurm
Worn out	ab geh tragah	ab geh tragen
Worry	saw re ah	sich sorgen
Worse	shlimmer	schlimmer
Worthless (man)	nun da day	Nutzlos
Wrap	ine vig lah	ein wickeln
wrap	viggle	wickeln
Wrench	schraubazeegel	Schraubenschlüsel
Wreath	granz	Kranz
Wring out	ausringa	ausringen
Wringer	ausringer	Ausringer
Write	schreib	Schreiben

Write	shreiba	Schreiben
Write	shrie vah	schreiben
Writing	schreibe	schreiben
Wrong	letz	falsch
Yacht	schiffla	Schiff
Yard	hof	Hof
Yardstick	longmess	Yardstock
Yeast	sotz	Hefe
Yellow	gehl	Gelb
Yes(do you agree)	gel	gell
Yesterday (day before)	for gescht	vorgestern
Yesterday	gesht	gestern
Yesterday	gey sh tar	gestern
Yet	noch	noch
Yet, however	doch	doch
Yoke	backholz	Joch
Yolk	doder	Dotter
Yolk	dough tar	Dotter
Young boy	cal	kind
Yours	dinahs	deins
Yours	diens	deins

Rev. Joseph Senger
2031 12th St. NW
Minot, ND 58703-0803

701-839-8927

August 22, 2011

DEAR THERESA,

HERZLICHEN DANK FOR THE UNBELIEVBLE BOOK.
OF GERMAN WORDS.

I THOUGHT IT WAS TO BE JUST A SMALL PAMPHLET. THIS
IS REALLY REMARKABLE. I JUST LOVE IT.

NO SUCH BOOK HAS EVER BEEN ATTEMPTED. PROFESSOR
STUMPH HAS A FEW WORDS IN HIS BOOK. BUT IT CANNOT
BE COMPARED TO YOURS.

THIS IS REALLY A MONUMENTAL WORK. HOW IMPORTANT FOR
THE PRESERVATION OF OUR LANGUAGE.

SOMEHOW IT SHOULD BE PUBLISHED AND SOLD IN GERMANY.
THE AVERAGE GERMAN HAS NO IDEA OF THESE WORDS.

WITH BEST WISHES FOR GOOD HEALTH, AND GOD'S BLESSINGS
I REMAIN

SINCERELY YOURS IN CHRIST,

REV JOSEPH SENGER

June 18, 2009

Theresa Wald
Grand Forks, North Dakota 58201

Dear Tyrase:

It is easy to observe and appreciate the work you did to compile this lexicon.

It will help preserve your german dialect for those with like interests.

Thomas N. Headland 6/18/09
Thomas N. Headland, Ph.d.
International Anthropology
 Consultant
Dallas, Texas, 75236-5629 USA

June 17, 2009

Theresa Wald
Grand Forks, No. Dak.

Dear Theresa:

It was good to have you attend the colloquium at the University of North Dakota.

The work you did to produce the lexicon on the German Dialect will be appreciated by all those who still speak the language, as well as future scholars of the language.

Of the 6,609 different languages in the world, the work you did must be accounted among them.

Sincerely,

Kenneth Rehg, Ph.D
International Linguist

Tyrase Wald received a Bachelor's degree from Minot State University in North Dakota and has credits from eight other institutions of higher learning, including universities in North Dakota, Minnesota, and Canada. Her focus of studies has been in the field of business, an area she has predominately worked in throughout her adult life.

She enjoys writing, painting, sewing, reading, weaving and painting. Wald's oil and acrylic paintings have been displayed at two art shows, one of them at *Lowe's Gardens*.

Wald is a member of the *Order Franciscans Secular* religious group and writes a column for that organization.

Theresa Wald has had poems published in *Prairie People's Magazine, Plainswoman, Inner Reflections, A College Poetry Anthology, Editor's Choice Series,* and *the International Library of Poetry*.

The author has traveled to eight different countries, visiting some of the countries in Grand Forks, ND.

"German My Way"'" is her eighth published book.

Tyrase and her father

www.ingramcontent.com/pod-product-compliance
Lightning Source LLC
Chambersburg PA
CBHW050754110526
44592CB00003B/57